GOSPEL REVOLUTION

JD GREEAR

Curriculum Developed by
JASON GASTON

GOSPEL REVOLUTION: Recovering the Power of Christianity

Student Book

Published by LifeWay Press®

©2012 J.D. Greear

ISBN: 978-1-4158-7691-6

Item: 005556935

Dewey Decimal Classification: 248.83

Subject Headings: CHRISTIAN LIFE \ DISCIPLESHIP \ INTERPERSONAL RELATIONS

All Scripture quotations are taken from the Holman Christian Standard Bible®, Copyright 1999, 2000, 2002, 2003, 2009 by Holman Bible Publishers. Used by permission.

To order additional copies of this resource, order online at *www.lifeway.com*.

Printed in the United States of America

Student Ministry Publishing

LifeWay Church Resources

One LifeWay Plaza

Nashville, TN 37234-0175

CONTENTS

About the Author 4

A Word from J.D. 5

Gospel Reading Plan 6

The Gospel Prayer 7

SESSION 1
Gospel Change 8

SESSION 2
Gospel Discovery 18

SESSION 3
Gospel Acceptance. 28

SESSION 4
Gospel Approval 38

SESSION 5
Gospel Response. 48

SESSION 6
Gospel Faith 58

SESSION 7
Substitute Gospels 68

SESSION 8
Gospel Depth. 78

ABOUT THE AUTHOR

At the age of 27, **J.D. Greear** became the pastor of a 40-year-old neighborhood church. In the 9 years since, that congregation of 400 has grown to over 5,000 in weekly attendance. Today, the Summit Church, located in Raleigh-Durham, NC, is recognized as one of the fastest growing churches in North America.

As a teacher, J.D.'s messages aren't intended to just show people how to live better lives. His goal is to leave people in awe of the amazing love of God. Because of his belief in the power of the gospel, J.D. has led the Summit to set a goal of planting more than 1,000 gospel-centered churches in the next 40 years.

J.D. holds a Ph.D. in Systematic Theology from the Southeastern Baptist Theological Seminary. He also lived and worked among Muslims in Southeast Asia for two years and wrote *Breaking the Islam Code*. J.D. & his beautiful wife Veronica have four ridiculously cute kids, Kharis, Alethia, Ryah, and Adon.

Unless God calls him elsewhere, J.D. plans on staying at the Summit Church until he preaches his last sermon at his own funeral before saying goodbye and hopping into the casket.

WELCOME TO A GOSPEL REVOLUTION!

For many years my Christianity seemed to consist of a list of things to do and not do. The result was spiritual frustration and weariness. Learning to dwell on the gospel changed all that. It produced in me the one thing religion could not: a *desire* for God.

The gospel is not just the way we begin in Christ; it is also the way we grow in Christ. Dwelling on the gospel produces freedom, joy, radical sacrifice, and audacious faith. The gospel has revolutionized my life, and it has revolutionized our church. I believe it will revolutionize yours, too.

In light of that, I'd like to encourage you to do a couple of things concurrently with this Bible study. For the next eight weeks, a) pray the four parts of the Gospel Prayer and b) read along with me through the four Gospels: Matthew, Mark, Luke, and John.

Why? Because I want you to saturate yourself in the gospel every day. The most gospel-centered books ever written are the Gospels. You'll find Jesus there. Dwell with Him in the Gospels for eight weeks, and let the Gospel Prayer saturate your heart and mind in His beauty and love. I think you'll never be the same.

Blessings to you as you begin your Gospel Revolution!

J.D. Greear

GOSPEL READING PLAN

Below is your 40-day Gospel Reading Plan, designed to begin after your first small-group meeting. To stay on track, you'll want to check off five reading sections per week.

	DAY	READING			DAY	READING	
☐	1	Matthew 1–2	Week 1	☐	21	Luke 5–6	Week 5
☐	2	Matthew 3–4		☐	22	Luke 7	
☐	3	Matthew 5–7		☐	23	Luke 8–9	
☐	4	Matthew 8–9		☐	24	Luke 10–11	
☐	5	Matthew 10–12		☐	25	Luke 12–13	
☐	6	Matthew 13–14	Week 2	☐	26	Luke 14–16	Week 6
☐	7	Matthew 15–16		☐	27	Luke 17–19	
☐	8	Matthew 17–18		☐	28	Luke 20–21	
☐	9	Matthew 19–20		☐	29	Luke 22–24	
☐	10	Matthew 21–23		☐	30	John 1–2	
☐	11	Matthew 24–25	Week 3	☐	31	John 3–4	Week 7
☐	12	Matthew 26–28		☐	32	John 5–6	
☐	13	Mark 1–3		☐	33	John 7–8	
☐	14	Mark 4–5		☐	34	John 9–10	
☐	15	Mark 6–7		☐	35	John 11–12	
☐	16	Mark 8–10	Week 4	☐	36	John 13–14	Week 8
☐	17	Mark 11–13		☐	37	John 15–16	
☐	18	Mark 14–16		☐	38	John 17	
☐	19	Luke 1–2		☐	39	John 18–19	
☐	20	Luke 3–4		☐	40	John 20–21	

The Gospel Prayer

"In Christ, there is nothing I can
do that would make You love me
more, and nothing I have done that
makes You love me less. Your presence
and approval are all I need for everlasting joy.
As You have been to me, so I will be to others.
As I pray, I'll measure Your compassion by the
cross and Your power by the resurrection."

SESSION 1:
GOSPEL CHANGE

Hear this truth loud and clear: God doesn't need anything from you. God wants the attention and affection of your heart.

Our goal this week will be to clearly define the gospel and discover what authentic gospel change looks like. The theme running rampant throughout the Scriptures is that God does not want our works, but rather the affections of our hearts. For most young believers, we're taught to stay busy doing church stuff. Our calendars get filled with Bible study groups, visitations, retreats, camps, pizza parties, mission trips, etc. And let's be honest, the majority of these religious activities are good! The truth is that the "busy Christian life" has become the biggest murderer of the gospel-centered life. The question in this session is simple: Are we trying to earn the love and affection of God by our works or are we living in the joy of God's love declared over us in the gospel?

Warm Up

If you've grown up going to church, what things do you associate with it? What comes to mind when considering your early years in the church? If you did not, what was your first impression, if any, of church?

What are some things about your past church experiences that are really funny, outdated, or just out of place?

What is the gospel in your own words?

The Christian Life

Below are a few questions to help us get started. We will come back to these questions in Week 8 to see how much change has taken place over the course of this study. You should think of this like the first day of weight training class in high school; though painful and a bit out of your comfort zone, good wisdom would say to evaluate your current standing to see where you are so you can celebrate later just how much you've changed and grown.

Write your answers in the space provided below.

Why did you, or why would you, want to become a Christian?

Describe Christian growth in your own words.

What do you hope to get out of this study over the next eight weeks?

Video Set Up

What comes to mind when you hear "gospel"? Many of us have some exposure to this word from church, media, or pop culture. But do any of us really get the significance the gospel could have on our everyday lives? Do we understand the power available to us in the gospel? In our first session, Jason Gaston introduces the concept of a gospel-centered life and how it unlocks the revolutionary power and joy we may be missing.

Video Guide: SESSION 1 "GOSPEL CHANGE"

The gospel gives us a brand new set of _____.

Two Ways of Seeing Change

1. Mechanical or Religious Change:

• Growth comes from _____ _____.

• Doing more, trying harder, being better.

2. Organic or Gospel Change:

The gospel tells you not to change in order to _____ the approval of God, but because you _____ the approval of God in Christ!

Gospel change works _____ the approval of God, not _____ the approval of God.

The gospel changes everything, even the way we change.

Video Feedback

The goal here is to talk about the video and to enhance your experience by hearing how God is using this teaching in the lives of others in your group.

If you could summarize the key point in this message, what would it be?

Come up with a tweetable key point. When your group is finished meeting, tweet/update your Facebook status with that key phrase (using the hashtag "#gospelrev").

From the notes you took during the video, what jumped out at you as something you've never heard before or challenged you?

What are some ways you have attempted to change mechanically?

In what ways does the gospel give you a new lens?

Jason mentioned that gospel change is "working from the approval of God rather than working for the approval of God." How does that statement sit with you? How does that affect the way you approach change?

Discussion Questions

If you were to describe your life as a Christian up to this point and the change that you've gone through, would you put yourself more in the "religious change" or the "gospel change" category? Why?

Look at the Apostle Paul's prayer for the believers in Ephesus in Ephesians 3:16-19. What was Paul asking of God on the people's behalf?

Why do you think Paul was praying above all for these specific things?

According to Paul, what does this prayer indicate is necessary and central to the life of a Christian?

Key Thought: The abundant well of the riches of God's grace and mercy will never run dry! The love of God, through Christ, is the most valuable thing that could ever saturate our hearts.

Although being a follower of Christ is supposed to be freeing, often times we feel like it's more of a burden. What do you find to be the most difficult part of being a Christian? How does the gospel bring a new perspective to that thought?

Wrap Up

In this session, we unpacked the foundation that this entire study is built upon. At the center of the Christian faith is not a set of rules to follow, but a gracious Father rescuing His children from death and giving them new life. Love for God is at the heart of Christianity. We do not serve a God who is a tyrant king who demands that we earn His acceptance, but a loving Father who gives us His acceptance in Christ.

How does your understanding of Christianity change based upon this truth?

Pray

In the space provided below, write your prayer to God. We are familiar with spoken prayers, but we often neglect to write out our prayers to the Lord. Each week we will close with a written prayer. After the study is complete, take time to look back over your prayers and notice how God is moving in your life.

Pray today that God would use His Word over the next several sessions to transform your heart, reveal sin, and help you see His glory!

The Family Tree: *Matthew 1*

Take just a few minutes and write out as much of your family tree as you can. Yes, we even want you to include your crazy uncle!

The opening chapter of the Gospel of Matthew begins with a look at Jesus' family tree. This family tree of Jesus includes some pretty amazing people, some with incredibly difficult names to pronounce, and also a few that the first century Jewish audience (those who are reading this account) would have been baffled by. Examples of some amazing people in that lineage include people like David and Abraham! These two guys were incredibly prominent men in the history of God's people. In fact, both of these guys were given promises by God that the Savior of the world would come from their family tree. With that in mind, it's fitting that those guys are included.

There are also those that would have made the "Not So Top Ten" list on the evening news. To the astonishment of everyone, Jesus' family tree included someone like Rahab (a prostitute)!

Think

What can you assume about God's kingdom when He includes someone like Rahab alongside people like Abraham and David in the lineage of Jesus?

Look at the angel's announcement (v. 21). What was to be Jesus' primary purpose in coming to the earth?

What does that mean to you?

Pray

Spend a few minutes thanking God for using not only great people in history to bring about our Savior, but also people that were a far cry from the best of the best. Thank God for His primary mission in coming to earth to rescue and redeem the lost! Thank Him for rescuing and redeeming you!

Fight Temptation with His Love: *Matthew 4*

Have you ever had a really great thing happen to you and then immediately had something really difficult happen? (example: went to summer camp and God did great things in your life, but then you got home and _____.)

In Matthew 4, Jesus just heard some amazing words that God the Father declared over Him (3:17), and now He was being led into the desert to spend some good quality time with Satan. WHAT? I can think of a lot more people I'd rather be in the desert with than Satan, that's for sure. As Jesus was in the wilderness, Satan used several different strategies to tempt Jesus. Do you know what motivation and strategy Jesus used in His defense? It was the words His Father had declared over Him. Because He was loved so much by His Father, the temptations of Satan lost their glamour and Jesus revealed them as the fraud that they were.

That's exactly how God the Father desires for you and I to fight temptation. He wants us to rest in the deep and unconditional love of the Father toward us!

Think

In what ways are you being tempted in your life right now?

To truly understand temptation, you have to realize what the temptation is promising. It always promises something it can't deliver. Based on what you just wrote above, try to figure out what the promise of each temptation is and think through why that is a lie.

How does the truth that God unconditionally loves you change the way you meet that temptation?

Pray

Thank God for your acceptance in Christ. Ask God to enlarge your heart and mind to a greater understanding of His love and acceptance of you! Allow His acceptance through Christ to empower you to live the life He has called you to live. No more living to gain His acceptance, rather begin living FROM His acceptance.

"How Should We Pray?": *Matthew 6*

This is the question the disciples asked Jesus. In truth, it is the real question that keeps so many people from developing rich prayer lives. Most people want to believe prayer works, but have no idea where to start. So when the need to pray arises, they offer up a skeptical but desperate plea to God to fix whatever is broken in their lives. Often, a lack of confidence in prayer turns into a mundane routine with little or no variance and little or no connection with God.

How did Jesus respond to this question? While the question by the disciples is recorded in Luke's account (Luke 11:1), the full response Christ gives is recorded in Matthew 6:1-13. We refer to this famous passage as "The Lord's Prayer," though it would be far more accurate to call it the disciples' prayer since this is Jesus' prescription for our prayer lives. A walk-through of this passage will hopefully free you to begin praying with confidence in the way God designed prayer to be practiced. When you pray:

Pray to an audience of One. Matthew 6:5-6

The heart matters, not the tongue. Matthew 6:7-8

Prayer is first God-centered. Matthew 6:9-10

Pray as if your life depends on it. Matthew 6:11-13

Of course, prayer flows out of a heart captivated by the gospel.

Think

Does your prayer life feel vibrant or mundane? Which of the four elements above is your weakest link? How will the gospel change your perspective?

How does praying impact the rest of your day?

Pray

There would be no better place to send you today than to Matthew 6:5-13. Pray like Christ called His disciples to pray. Don't just recite it though. The psalmist's prayer in Psalm 19:14 was, "May the words of my mouth and the meditation of my heart be acceptable to You, Lord, my rock and my Redeemer." Meditate on these words. Let them become your words from your mind and heart, not just words on a page. Then pray them back to God.

God's love. Are you trying to earn it or allowing it to empower your life? Write your answer below and begin thinking of ways to allow His love to transform your life instead of spending your time trying to earn it.

What are you doing with God's love?

GOSPEL DISCOVERY

"Is your heart captivated by the glory and beauty of God? Are you overcome by a sense of awe and drawn in by a feeling of intimacy?"

Our sense of sight often determines our desires. In turn, our desires drive our decisions. If a bowl shows up in front of me and within it lies two scoops of vanilla ice cream, chunks of cookie dough drizzled with chocolate, and topped with whip cream and a cherry, you can count me in. If, however, that same bowl shows up in front of me with ice cream that smells like sour milk, dry cat food scattered all over it, and topped with peas and carrots, you can count me out. Our desires are driven by sight.

In the same way, my spiritual senses, namely spiritual sight, inform my beliefs. The apostle Paul called this spiritual sight the eyes of the heart. What I sense to be most valuable, most beautiful, and most desirable is what I will position my life to obtain. Paul's prayer, which must become our prayer, is that we begin to see the beauty of Christ above all things!

This week we will take a few more steps into our understanding of the beauty and power of the gospel. We will see in Isaiah 6 how Isaiah was overwhelmed by the size, holiness, and grace of God. What Isaiah saw changed the entire trajectory of his life.

Warm Up

What is something that you have seen that you'll never forget?

What about it makes you believe that you'll never forget it?

Weekly Review

Last week we began our study about the revolutionary power of the gospel. Jason taught about the difference between religious change and gospel-centered change. We saw that what Christ is after most is not our works, but our hearts. As our hearts are changed to desire Him more, our lives begin to change as a result.

How did your personal study of Matthew 1-12 go? What are some things you remember from your reading?

Did you have any "aha!" moments this week where the principles of change came to life for you?

Did you have any moments this week where you were reminded of these principles of change? How was your approach altered as a result?

Video Set Up

The gospel message is not just a few verses that come from the New Testament. The gospel is the grand story of God's salvation that runs throughout every page of the entire Bible. From the beginning to the end, the love of God for His children is intended to be the motivation for obedience to Him. In this session, Jason works through the Scriptures to build on last week's idea of gospel change.

Video Guide: SESSION 2 "Gospel Discovery"

1. God gave Isaiah a glimpse of His unimaginable _____.

2. God showed Isaiah His untouchable _____.

3. Isaiah experienced God's unexplainable _____.

The Gospel Example:

Life raft vs. dead in the water

Write your understanding of this example:

God wants to do something great _____ you before He does

something great _____ you.

Video Feedback

The goal here is to talk about the video and to enhance your experience by hearing how God is using this teaching in the lives of others in your group.

Jason stated in the video that many people try to define the gospel in several different ways. How did the analogy of the life raft vs. dead in the water resonate with you?

How does that illustration of the gospel give us a new lens for life?

If you could summarize the key point of this message in a tweet, what would it say?

Come up with a tweetable key point, and when your group is finished meeting, tweet/update your Facebook status with that key phrase (using the hashtag "#gospelrev").

Jason mentioned that Isaiah saw the unimaginable size of God in this passage. Describe a time where you have experienced this in your life.

If God wants to do something great in you before He does something great through you, how does that change the way you approach your day-to-day walk with Christ?

Discussion Questions

1. In Isaiah 6:1-2, Isaiah describes his encounter of the unimaginable size of God. What are some of the descriptions he gives?

2. In what ways is God completely different than everyone else? How is He set apart?

3. How did Isaiah's glimpse of God change him?

4. Look at Hebrews 12:1-2. The author uses the language "keeping our eyes on Jesus," emphasizing Jesus as a focal point for our life. Since you cannot see Jesus physically standing before you, what do you think it looks like in your everyday life for you to keep your eyes on Him?

5. In your life, what is most likely to distract you from keeping your eyes on Jesus? Why do you think it has so much influence over you?

6. How could your daily routine change to allow you to focus more on Christ this week?

Wrap Up

In this session, we looked at how the gospel story is told across the pages of Scripture. Jesus is the focal point whom we are to fix our eyes on at all times. Once you catch a glimpse of the greatness of God and discover the beauty of His grace through Christ, you are set free to live a life led by the Spirit. God doesn't force change upon us. He simply loves us and His love changes us on the inside which results in change on the outside.

Pray

In continuing along with our discipline of written prayers, spend a few minutes thinking about and responding to the truth that God desires to do something great in you before He does something great through you. Has God done something great in you yet? Pray that God would reveal areas of your life that are hindering you from fully embracing His love.

Same Seed, Different Soils: *Matthew 13:1-23*

Have you ever worked to grow anything (a summer garden, a bed of flowers, a bean in a plastic cup in elementary school)? Did you just plant it and leave it or did you tend to it? How did you feel when you finally saw it start to grow?

In Matthew 13, Jesus comes up with a story in his head and tells it to the people around Him in order to make a point. Making up these stories, or Parables, is one of the things Jesus did best when teaching His followers. He gives the picture of a guy who plants a seed in 4 types of soil. He then immediately follows the story by explaining what it meant to His disciples. He explains that some people will hear the word of God but not understand it. This is like the seeds that fell upon the rocks and never got planted in soil. Some people will hear the gospel and accept it immediately, only to waver in their faith when tough times come. This is like the seeds that are planted among rocky soil and are unable to develop roots. Some people will hear the gospel and have true affection for it, but it will be choked out by the things of this world. This is similar to how a plant can be choked out by thorns. Lastly, Jesus explains that people who hear the Word, understand it, and bear fruit will be like the seed that is planted in good soil.

Jesus makes it clear that the enemies of the gospel are Satan himself, believers not understanding the trials that will come as a result of following Jesus, and the distractions that come through the cares of this world.

Think

What is the difference in each situation? Was it the type of seed or was it the soil?

Almost all soil had a good response to the gospel at first. Does that worry you at all? What is the evidence of good soil?

In what areas of your life are you not allowing the gospel to take root in? Are there areas that you really don't want the gospel to go? How does this passage challenge that?

Pray

Take a few minutes and thank God for the opportunity that you've had to hear and understand the gospel. Pray also for the millions of people who are yet to hear the gospel and have this seed planted in them. Pray that God would immediately show you where the gospel is not allowed in your life.

Storm the Gates: *Matthew 16:13-20*

What's the difference between offense and defense? In sports, if you don't know which one you are on, you can end up going the wrong direction. In war, you wouldn't know whether to have your sword out or your shield up. It's important to know the difference.

In Matthew 16:13-20 we see a huge turning point for Jesus's disciples. Jesus asked, "Who do people say that the Son of Man is?" To His disciples, it probably seemed like Jesus was trying to feel out what culture was saying about Him. He could have been checking up on His street cred so the disciples immediately respond with the common, cultural answers. Jesus then makes it personal by asking who the disciples say He is. Peter's confession of Christ as the Messiah, the Christ, and the Son of the living God in verse 15 is crucial to this story.

After this confession, Jesus says that the confession of Christ as Lord is what His church will be built on and that the gates of hell won't be able to stand against it. What do gates do? Are they an offensive or defensive weapon? That's right. Hell is on the defensive in relation to the gospel. That's a game changer. The gospel in on the offense and hell is trying to lock up its doors.

Think

Do you believe that the gospel truly is more powerful than the things of this world? Do you believe that the church, based on the power of the gospel, is on the offense and that hell won't be able to stand up to it?

Does your life and your day-to-day actions line up with the belief that you are on the offense? Not only are you not on defense, but if you belong to Christ you are not on the sidelines either. You are in the game, this is a real war, and you need to know your role.

How does the truth that you are on offense and in a war change your view on evangelism and reaching your friends for Christ? Do you live like the gospel is true?

Pray

Pray that God will keep the gospel readily on your heart and mind and that you would use it like a weapon in your own life against the devil. Pray for the salvation of your family members and friends so that they can experience the hope that you have in Christ. Pray that God will mold you and your church into messengers of the gospel that attack the gates of hell.

Forgiven and Forgiving: *Matthew 18:23-35*

Have you ever owed someone something that you thought you could never repay? Maybe your parents replaced that car that you wrecked or you cracked your friend's phone. Did you feel overwhelmed? Sick? Anxious?

In Matthew 18, Jesus tells a parable about a man who owes a wealthy king 10,000 talents. One talent equaled 20 years' wages, so this was more money than this guy would ever make in the rest of his lifetime. This guy was in deep. This usually meant that the guy would have to be the king's slave. But in a crazy turn of events, the king completely wiped the debt clean. He tells the man not to worry. Jesus then says that the man who had be forgiven of the debt went outside, saw a guy who owed him a very small amount, and had him thrown in jail for not repaying what he owed. Jesus' listeners had to have thought that this was completely unreasonable. But remember the point of parables; they are to display one point. The point here is that if we understood all that we have been forgiven from God, we would not have any problem forgiving people who have done us wrong.

Think

Do you hold grudges? Can you think of that one specific grudge that you won't let go of? How does understanding the gospel challenge your right to hold this grudge?

Make a list of people you need to forgive or extend forgiveness to. Write out the offense you have against them. Compare those offenses against the ones you had toward God and what it cost Him to forgive you.

Pray

While forgiveness is not easy or natural, it is at the core of the Christian life. You became a Christian through an act of forgiveness towards you. Pray that God would give you a fresh awareness of the forgiveness that He has shown you. Pray that this awareness would push you to forgive others who have done wrong towards you.

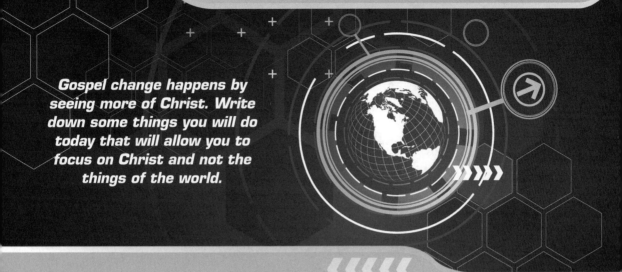

Gospel change happens by seeing more of Christ. Write down some things you will do today that will allow you to focus on Christ and not the things of the world.

Are you allowing your eyes to be pulled away from or fixed upon Christ?

GOSPEL ACCEPTANCE

"In Christ, there is nothing I can do that would make You love me more, and nothing I have done that makes You love me less."

The Gospel Prayer, Part 1

The gospel is the reality that God's complete acceptance is given to us once for all as a gift in Christ. Christ took our place as sinners and died the death that we deserved. In return, we get to take His place as sons and daughters and receive all the rights and privileges that were due unto Him. The gospel is "Jesus in my place." God could not love us any more than He does right now because He could not love Christ any more than He does right now and we are in Christ!

I remember one year in high school I put money into a broken vending machine. Of course, the machine took my money but gave me nothing in return. So, I did what any normal teenager would do, I did the gentle "bump" of the machine with my hip. Once that didn't work, I began thrust my shoulder into the side of the machine. After that failed, I resorted to kicking it. Nothing worked. It was a broken machine and there was no way to fix it.

The same is true of how we often come to God. We think if we come to God in a certain way with a certain posture and attitude we can control how He responds to us. We desperately want to control the love and acceptance of God toward us. The gospel declares love over our state of helplessness. This week is all about learning to live in light of God's amazing grace.

Warm Up

Have you ever been in a situation where you had to cover for someone (example: maybe you took the blame for a brother or a sister for something they did)? How did that turn out?

What is the best gift you've ever received? Why?

Weekly Review

Last week, Jason taught us about the size, holiness, and grace of God that Isaiah experienced in Isaiah 6. We saw that it was the exposure to who God really is that catapulted Isaiah's lifelong obedience. This past week we read through Matthew 13-23 where we encountered Jesus' parables and teachings on what a life focused on Christ looks like. We ended our reading with the greatest commandment where Christ summed up the law as loving God and loving others. It is the love of God that is the driving force in how we live in every aspect of our lives.

How did your reading this past week of Matthew 13-23 go? What did God teach you?

Over the past week, has any area of your life been affected by what we are learning so far in this study? If yes, explain.

Video Set Up

In this session we begin to unpack the Gospel Prayer. An important thing to understand about the prayer is this: when God looks at us, He sees Jesus! We will also take a look at the way the Enemy attempts to get us to doubt the love and acceptance of God towards us in Christ.

Video Guide: SESSION 3 "Gospel Acceptance"

Religion focuses on _____ change. The gospel focuses on the _____.

With religion, we obey to get something _____ God. The gospel changes us so we obey because we _____ God.

With religion, we change to _____ the approval of God. In the gospel, we change because we _____ the approval of God.

In Christ, there is _____ I can do that would make God love me more and nothing I have done that makes Him love me _____.

2 Corinthians 5:21: Jesus in my place!

The Enemy wants you to doubt your _____.

Matthew 3

Your identity is not on your ability to _____, but in the performance of _____ on your behalf.

Video Feedback

The goal here is to talk about the video and to enhance your experience by hearing how God is using this teaching in the lives of others in your group.

In what ways has the Enemy attacked your identity in the past?

If you are a child of God, do you even truly understand who you are?

Have you ever thought of the gospel as Jesus in your place? How does that change your approach to God?

In what ways have you sought to find your identity in your ability to perform?

Jason said that "religion obeys to get something from God, but the gospel says we obey because we love God." In what ways have you used God to get something you want?

Come up with a tweetable key phrase you think your friends need to hear. Take a minute and tweet/update your Facebook status with that key phrase (using the hashtag "#gospelrev").

Discussion Questions

Take a look at Matthew 4:1-11. Multiple times in this passage Satan says, "If you are the son of God." Why do you think Satan attacked Jesus' identity this way?

In what areas of your life does Satan attempt to get you to doubt your identity as a son/daughter in Christ?

How did Jesus respond to Satan? How does Jesus' response encourage you as you deal with those same accusations?

According to 2 Corinthians 5:17-21, God has made us new creations because of the work of Christ on our behalf. We are also called to be ambassadors for Christ everywhere we go. What should be your motivation for obedience as an ambassador (hint: it's at the end of this passage)?

Read Philippians 2:4-8. What does this passage tell us about Jesus' identity? In what ways does His confidence in His identity create a model for us to follow?

Wrap Up

In this session, we unpacked the first part of the Gospel Prayer. We looked at how God's acceptance of us through Christ should well up within us a deep love for God that religion simply cannot. We also learned the primary way Satan attacks believers is to get them to doubt their identity in Christ.

Pray

Spend the last minutes together as a group in prayer focused around the first part of the Gospel Prayer:

"In Christ, there is nothing I can do that would make You love me more and nothing I have done that makes You love me less."

Write in the space below your prayer of thanksgiving for this truth.

Value Christ and Don't Lose Sight: *Matthew 26:6-12*

Is there something that you would give anything to gain or you would give up anything to keep? What is that thing that you think you need in order to be happy or feel significant? Was there one thing that you thought of in response to each of these questions?

In Matthew 26, Jesus sits down to eat dinner at Simon the Leper's house. That's right. Jesus, the Son of God, is eating dinner with a leper. It is probably a whole group of lepers. These are the folks that people stayed away from, but Jesus sits down to eat with them.

In the middle of this dinner, a woman named Mary, who had seen Jesus raise her brother from the dead, takes a jar of very expensive perfume and pours it on Jesus' head. This was about a year's wages and she is pouring it out over His head. Jesus' disciples think that He should explain that they could use that money for ministry. Jesus replies to His disciples in verses 10-12. He explains that Mary is the only one who remembers who Jesus is. Christ reminds them that He is worth the cost of this perfume and He is worth everything that she owns. He is worth her most prized possessions and she was right to give them up for him.

Think

Mary gladly gave up her most prized possession because she saw Jesus as much more valuable than anything she owned. What is competing for your affection for Christ right now?

What is the one thing that you would have a tough time giving up?

What are you doing to remind yourself daily that Jesus is more valuable than any of your possessions or activities?

Pray

It is so easy to get caught up in day-to-day life and lose sight of the value of Christ. Praise God that though you may lose sight of Christ, He never loses sight of you or values you less than He did when He went to the cross for you. As you pray, ask God to help you keep Christ central in your life.

Be a Disciple: *Matthew 28:18-20*

Have you ever been dedicated to something that you loved (a team, a group, a person)? Were you able to recognize when people around you didn't have the same dedication? How did it make you feel to see the difference in those who were dedicated and those who weren't? Was there a reason that you were so invested in this?

Matthew 28 comes after the most traumatic events in any of the disciples' lives. They have given up everything to follow Jesus, only to have Him be taken away and crucified. Now, Jesus has risen from the dead and He has a message for His disciples. The final message from Jesus to His disciples is essentially this: "As you go, make disciples and teach them everything that I have spent the last years teaching you". The great commission is often seen as a missional text where Jesus tells them to "go". While that is true, what is altogether more important is to understand what they are supposed to do while they go. Jesus is calling them to make disciples.

The call to make disciples only makes sense if you remember what they just went through. They just witnessed Jesus die on a cross and rise again. When Christ defeated death by walking out of the tomb, the hope of the world was made new once again. There is no fear and there is a hope that has never been seen before. Without this, there is no reason to make disciples. The resurrection gives us both a hope and a confidence.

Think

Would you characterize yourself more as a fan or a follower of Jesus? Why?

In what areas of your life do you find the most joy in following Christ?

In what areas of your life do you ignore Christ's commands most often? What causes you to do this?

Pray

If Christ hadn't risen from the dead, Christians would be the most hopeless people on the planet. Take time and thank God for Christ's on the Cross and His resurrection. Pray that you would recognize the power you have been given through Christ's victory on the cross. Pray that you would seek to grow as a disciple of Jesus and not just a fan.

More Than You Could Ask or Imagine: *Mark 2:1-12*

Have you ever had a need and prayed to God about it? Did God answer it in the way that you expected Him to? In the end, was His answer more or less sufficient for what you had originally needed?

Mark 2:1-12 is the natural result of Jesus healing numerous people. People all over the area had heard of what Jesus had done, and it naturally drove people to action. In this specific case, people who had heard of Jesus' power, brought one of their paralytic friends to see Jesus. Their logic is pretty simple: Jesus heals people. Our friend needs to be healed. Lets take him to Jesus.

When this man shows up to be healed, Jesus offers another solution. Jesus looks at him and in response to the faith of his friends, says "Son, your sins are forgiven" (v. 5). Jesus met this man's needs in a way that he wasn't expecting. Jesus did more than the man knew he needed. Jesus was showing that the point of His ministry wasn't physical healing, but it was much bigger than that. Jesus met spiritual needs and met all other needs all the more abundantly.

Think

What are the things that you are asking God for right now?

The paralytic and his friends are great examples of faith. Do you really believe that God is able to do what you are asking Him to do?

If God were to say no or delay your request, would you be okay with that? How do you trust God in these areas?

Pray

As you pray, thank God for people who stand in faith beside you. Pray that God would open your eyes to see His power through the resurrection and His compassion for you through the cross. Pray that God would expand your view of Him and see that He is powerful enough to do more than you could ever ask or imagine.

The approval of God is yours in Christ. Take a few minutes and think through all the things you are doing to try and earn His approval. Now think about the freedom that should be found in having His approval because of Christ.

Since I can't earn God's approval, what should motivate my actions?

SESSION 4:
GOSPEL APPROVAL

"Your presence and approval are all I need for everlasting joy."
Gospel Prayer, Part 2

Cheating happens in all different shapes and sizes. In sports it may take on the form of using performance-enhancing drugs to give yourself the edge over your opponent. In academics it may look like you pulling out your phone during a test and looking up the answer to something on the Internet. It also happens in relationships. In marriage, we call it adultery. Adultery is when a person finds intimacy with someone other than their spouse. Here's the crazy thing: in our relationship with God, we often act like adulterers. We look for joy, happiness, approval, and contentment in other things and people rather than in God Himself. In those moments, we are pursuing idols. The moment we think something—anything—will satisfy us better than God, we become idolaters. This week, let's take a look at our lives and see how, even when we didn't intend to do it, we've allowed idols to creep in.

Warm Up

Take a few minutes and talk about the thing that dominates most of your free time during the week (do not include homework, class, or even work.) Do you enjoy or despise that thing? Why do you continue doing it?

If you had a pass from your parents and a "get out of school free card" for one year, what would be the one thing you would go and do (travel, live in a cave, etc.).?

Weekly Review

Last week, we unpacked the first part of the Gospel Prayer, which really hammers home at our self-righteousness. We saw how in the gospel, God cannot love us any more or any less than He does right now. If you are a Christian, you are hidden in Christ so that when God looks at us, He only sees Christ in us! We learned that Satan's number one strategy is to attack our identity in Christ, attempting to get us to doubt our right standing before God. If you are tracking with the reading plan laid out in this study, you encountered the death, burial and resurrection of Christ at the end of the Gospel of Matthew. You also saw the significance of the miracle-filled ministry of Christ in the opening chapters of the gospel of Mark.

Did God use the teaching from last week to help you deal with any questions that you may have about your relationship with God?

Congratulations, you've read through an entire Gospel already! After reading Matthew in a short period of time, did anything major stand out to you? Did you notice anything about Jesus that you may have never seen before?

Video Set Up

In session 4 we are going to study the second part of the Gospel Prayer, where we will see how the gospel confronts the idols of our lives. Jason will talk to us about how our hearts are hard wired toward idols, and often times we are blind to them! We'll also be taking an Idolatry Detector Test so we can take a look at where we may have built some idols. Here's the great news; no matter how deep our idolatry goes, the gospel goes deeper and proves to us that God is better than any idols we've put in His place.

Video Guide: SESSION 4 "Gospel Approval"

Your _____ and _____ are all I need for everlasting joy.

Kabod: (Hebrew) "glory" or "_____."

An idol is not necessarily a bad thing. It can be a good thing that you give "_____" weight to.

We've made secondary things primary. See Romans 1:25.

God, I know you're good, but if you would only give me _____, I promise I'll do whatever you want.

Whatever is in that blank for you has become your idol.

The love and pursuit of idols in our hearts will fade when the _____ becomes greater.

Jesus isn't after a better morality. He's after the _____ of your heart.

Video Feedback

The goal here is to talk about the video and to enhance your experience by hearing how God is using this teaching in the lives of others in your group.

Idolatry Test:

When you worry, what is it usually about?

The thing you're most worried about losing is _____.

If you could change one thing about your life right now, what would it be?

When you have been the happiest in your life, what was going on that made you feel that way (relationship, athletic success, etc.)?

Have you ever felt depressed? If so, what made you feel that way?

What is the one thing you are most willing to sacrifice for?

Where do you turn for comfort?

Look at your answers to the idolatry test. Did anything surprise you or stand out to you that you'd be willing to share with the group?

How have you experienced Jesus as better and more fulfilling than the things you've put in His place? Can you give a specific example?

If you could summarize the key point of this message in a tweet, what would it say?

Come up with a tweetable key point, and when your group is finished meeting, tweet/update your Facebook status with that key phrase (using the hashtag "#gospelrev").

Discussion Questions

1. What are some of the things that you might be giving a "God type weight" to in your life? Remember, these might not be things you would consider bad. How have you given that type of weight to them?

2. Look at Exodus 20:1-6. What is the first commandment that God gave the people of Israel? Why do you think that was important? What does that commandment say about the character of God?

3. 1 Timothy 6:11: Jason referred to this as the "flee and follow" passage in the video. Why is it important that you pursue Christ when you flee from idols? Explain.

4. Romans 8:35-39 is a great passage on God's unending love for His people. Take a moment and circle the words in this passage that would threaten your relationship with God. Now underline the phrase that cements your hope in the gospel. Discuss what this passage says about God's love for us.

5. What are some practical things you can do to "follow Christ" when you are "fleeing from sin"? This is a great opportunity for you to share as a group some things that you guys can do together for accountability.

Wrap Up

In this session we explored how we are often tempted to look to things other than God to find happiness and security. The Idolatry test gave us a glimpse into some of the hidden idols we have in our lives. The most important thing we did in this session was to fix our eyes on Jesus, who displays over and over again that His love and presence are all we need for joy! The presence and approval of Christ is all we need for everlasting joy. As we move into the second half of the Gospel Revolution, we must do so knowing that our joy is in Christ!

Pray

Spend the last minutes of your time together asking God to continue to give you sensitivity to the Holy Spirit as He points out areas of your life where you are seeking joy and approval in things/people other than Him! Record your prayer in the space below.

See It All: *Mark 10*

In Mark 10:17-23, we read the account of a young guy who apparently heard Jesus was the way to eternal life and wanted to find out more about it. We see that he was a very rich and successful guy and that he had good standing in the society. This made it very surprising and a sign of great humility that he would kneel before Jesus.

Jesus, knowing the man's heart, begins to ask him some questions to dig deeper into his life. He first reminds him of the Ten Commandments which of course, being a good Jew, the rich man knew and says he has kept. Jesus then, knowing that rules cannot save him, gets to the heart of the issue. He looks on the guy and out of love reveals to him that he has an idol, his wealth. He is looking to something else, other than God, for his ultimate satisfaction and acceptance. Now don't miss this! It doesn't appear that this guy was an evil businessman who got rich by stepping on others on his way to the top. He sought out Jesus, tried to do good things; he even knelt before Jesus. The problem was that the rich, young ruler was only willing to let Jesus have control over some of his life. He wanted to hold onto his earthly security, money and power, while using God to get eternal security. Jesus loved him too much to allow him to hold onto earthly riches which He knew would destroy the young ruler.

The gospel always addresses our idols, even ones that no one else knows about or the ones that are accepted by society. Even though it may be painful, God loves us enough to tear them down so that in Him, we can have the joy and acceptance we are really seeking.

Think

The rich young man cared more about his wealth than anything else in his life. What in your life do you give more significance to than God? (friends, acceptance, grades, popularity, stuff)?

Now that you have identified some of the idols in your own heart, what are some steps that you could take to remove them from your life?

Pray

Ask God to reveal the areas in your life you are valuing more than Christ. Spend some time confessing to God these idols in your heart. Remember that in Christ you are accepted and made clean. Pray that you will begin finding pleasure and acceptance in Him rather than any other places.

Be Ready: *Mark 13*

From the beginning of time, people have debated when and how the world is going to end. From Nostradamus's predictions to the Mayan calendar to theories of global warming and giant asteroids hitting the earth, many people and civilizations have had ideas about when the world would end. Apparently they were happening while Jesus was on earth as well because He addresses the question in Mark 13:32-37. He begins by telling us no one, other than the Father, knows when the world will come to an end, not even Himself. In other words, quit worrying about when it will happen. God knows and He's got it under control. Instead Jesus tells us we should start talking about how we should live, knowing one day that it will happen. Jesus basically says we should live ready.

So, what does living ready look like? First, it does not mean that we ignore the problems of this world and those around us because "it's all gonna burn anyway." This world is God's and all that is in it and we are to take care of our Father's creation that He has entrusted to us. Living ready means that we are constantly aware of the mission God has entrusted us with and the reality that only His Kingdom and our investment in it will remain. In other words, continue to work hard and purse good grades, a family, a career, etc., and then use the blessings God has given you to serve Him and others in your life.

Think

If Jesus were to show up at your front door right now, would you be ready? Why or why not?

How do Jesus' words give you a peace about the end of the world we know will one day come? How can you share and show that peace to a world who often worries about the end of the world?

Pray

When Christ returns, all of the brokenness and sadness in the world will be healed. God will restore everything and sickness, pain and death will be no more. Thank God that despite the pain and fear that is in the world now, we have a hope and a promise that it will one day pass away. Ask God to show you ways that in light of the riches we have in heaven, you can be generous with your lives now.

The Death of Jesus: *Mark 15*

Have you ever thought about how weird it is that we celebrate the day Christ died on the cross as Good Friday? Almost no death is ever a good thing. But Jesus' death was different than most. Where most people die as a result of their own sin, Jesus lived a perfect life. Jesus willingly took our sin on Himself and paid the penalty that we deserved. This is the good news of the gospel. Before Christ, we stood in relationship to God as enemies. We chose to go our own way over God's and the result was a life bound for death. Jesus rescued us from this death and took our place. He took our sin and we got His righteousness.

Mark 15 records the death of Jesus on the cross. As we just saw, the death of Jesus was good because it was for our benefit. That is the gospel in four words: Jesus in my place. Jesus endured mocking from the crowd, a beating from the guards and being nailed to the cross, all for us. Near the end of the chapter, verse 38 tells us the curtain of the temple was torn apart. The curtain separated the people from the presence of God because man, being sinful, could not enter God's presence. When Jesus' body was broken for us, He allowed us a way safely into the presence of God. The curtain is now torn because we are now allowed into God's presence. We have been restored as adopted sons and daughters of the Father.

Think

What stands out to you as you read Mark's account of Jesus' crucifixion?

Does the story of Jesus' death bring about strong emotions in you (anger, sadness, joy) or have you heard it so many times that it has lost its effectiveness? Ask God to help make the story fresh and important to you again as you think about the extent of His sufferings.

In your own words, describe the death of Jesus and why it is important to you. Say these words out loud to God.

Pray

When Jesus died on the cross, God's love and perfect justice were magnificently put on display. God punished sin by taking it on Himself and allowed us to come back to Him once again. As you think about the cross, thank God for giving Jesus as a sacrifice in our place. Ask God to give us eyes to see how great a sacrifice it was for the Perfect Son of God to do this. Ask for the joy and humility that comes from knowing while there was nothing we could do to get back to God, Jesus did it for us.

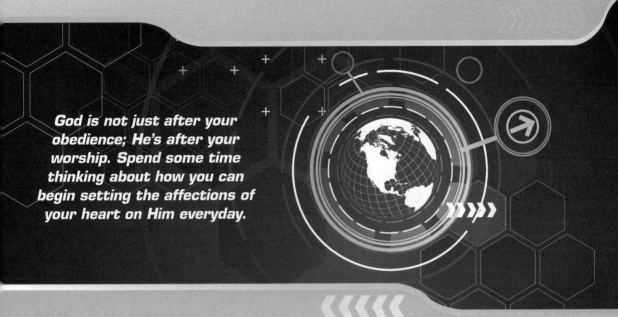

God is not just after your obedience; He's after your worship. Spend some time thinking about how you can begin setting the affections of your heart on Him everyday.

How are you worshiping God during the week?

SESSION 5:
GOSPEL RESPONSE

"As you have been to me, so I will be to others." The Gospel Prayer, Part 3

In October 2000, Warner Bros. released the film, *Pay It Forward*. The movie tracked the spread of the generosity-centered, viral movement from its inception as an 11-year-old boy's class project to its eventual influence over our entire nation. Tasked with finding a way to change the world for the better, the 11-year-old boy devised a charitable pyramid scheme where the recipient of one favor then does one favor for three separate third parties instead of simply returning the favor.

When we experience the benefit of someone's generosity toward us, it challenges us, and calls for a response in some capacity. Do we pay them back? Do we thank them and go about our business? Do we pay it forward? The only thing we cannot do is ignore this generosity!

The generosity extended toward us in the gospel is beyond comprehension, and our only choice is to live a life of radical generosity in response. We love because we have been loved. We forgive because we have been forgiven much. The grace of God toward us has been the driving force for the church's mission for 2,000 years and it will be the fuel for the mission until Christ's return.

Warm Up

Talk about an instance where someone did a random act of kindness toward you. Maybe you have a great story of how you did a random act of kindness toward a stranger or a friend. Describe the experience.

Can you remember a time when you extended grace toward someone when it wasn't very easy or fun to do? What were your emotions like during that time? Did you find it difficult or easy? What were your feelings afterward?

Weekly Review

Last week we unpacked the second part of the Gospel Prayer that says "Your presence and approval are all I need for everlasting joy." We were created to find our joy and approval in God, but we've looked for it in so many other places other than Him, which is what we call idolatry. Jason talked to us about the idols of our hearts, and that the only way those idols begin to fade and lose their luster is when the gospel becomes bigger and more attractive!

Learning to confront our idols is key to growing as a follower of Christ. After last week's session, were you made aware of any more idols in your life? Would you like to share them with the group?

You have been praying the Gospel Prayer now for a few weeks. How is God using that in your life as you seek to follow Him?

Video Set Up

In this session, Jason will be teaching through Part 3 of the Gospel Prayer that emphasizes living a life of radical generosity in response to the generosity that we have been shown by God through Christ in the gospel. You will want to make sure you pay close attention to the difference between guilt-driven motivations of generosity and grace-based motivations of generosity.

Video Guide: SESSION 5 "Gospel Response"

1. As you have been to _____ so I will be to

_____.

Guilt-Driven Generosity vs. Grace-Based Generosity (2 Cor. 8:9)

2. Paul motivates not by _____ but by _____.

As you have been to me (Eph. 2:1-9)

3. The generosity of God toward us also changes our attitude towards our

_____.

4. God not only _____ us in the gospel, but He

_____ us with the gospel.

Video Feedback

The goal here is to talk about the video and to enhance your experience by hearing how God is using this teaching in the lives of others in your group.

Which teaching point from Jason in the video stood out to you the most? Why?

If you could summarize the key point in this message in a tweet, what would it be? Take a minute and tweet/update your Facebook status with that key phrase (using the hashtag "#gospelrev").

In what ways have you been motivated by guilt-driven generosity?

The third part of the Gospel Prayer is "As you have been to me, so I will be to others." Take a few minutes and share with the group some of the ways that God has "been to you."

How does the generosity of God change your attitude toward your possessions?

Discussion Questions

1. Read Ephesians 2:1-9. Take a few minutes and talk about the generosity of God toward us through Christ that is portrayed in this passage (as you have been to me).

2. We all know people who we feel have wronged us in some capacity, and we want to get back at them. Paul speaks to exactly this mind-set in Romans 12:19-21. What does he mean by "heaping fiery coals"? How can the gospel be our fuel for choosing grace over revenge?

3. Read Acts 2:44-47. The early church that is portrayed in the Book of Acts had some faults, just like we do. But those people loved to take care of each other, and they did so regularly. In fact, they loved each other so well that those in their community began to take notice. Their generosity spilled out into a watching world. How did the early church care for one another? How could your group put the generosity of Christ on display in your schools/circles of influence?

4. Take a few minutes and, as a group, come up with a game plan to intentionally display the generosity of Christ to those in your schools/circles of influence. Use the space below to write down a few options and then select one to focus on.

Wrap Up

In this session, we looked at how the gospel creates in us a grace-motivated life of generosity toward others! The bigger the gospel becomes in our lives, the more generous we become with our time, talents, and treasures. God saves us in the gospel and sends us as ambassadors of His generosity to a world that is still dead in sin. As He has been to us, so we shall be to others!

What is one thought you need to remember from your discussion time? Write it down so you won't forget it.

Pray

Take a few minutes to pray through this part of the Gospel Prayer. Write down your prayer, focusing on this phrase, *"As you have been to me, so I will be to others."* How does this part of the Gospel Prayer impact you?

Love Your Enemies: *Luke 6*

In Luke 6:27-36, we read Jesus' teaching on how we are to treat those who treat us poorly. In His teaching, we see a radical departure from the rest of the world on how we are to treat our enemies. Where most would say we should treat others how they have treated us, Jesus reverses this mind-set and tells us to do good to even those who have treated us badly. The world says if someone takes something from you, they should give it back. Jesus says we should let them keep it and ask them what else they need.

This was not just a teaching for Jesus, but the way He lived His life. When we were rebelling against Him, He came to show love to the world knowing He would be rejected and nailed to a cross. Even while on the cross He said, "Father, forgive them, because they do not know what they are doing" (Luke 23:34). Now as followers of Christ, Jesus calls us to follow His example and be merciful just as our Father is merciful.

Think

Who are you upset with right now because of how they have treated you? Are you willing to let it go in light of what Christ has done for us?

Why is forgiveness difficult for you to give? How does our forgiveness in Christ enable us to forgive others?

In your own words, write out how God has been merciful to you. Start with what Jesus has done and go from there.

Pray

Spend some time asking God to help you understand how great His love was that He would forgive us at the cost of His only son. Now when He looks at you, He sees you as His own child. Ask that He would allow that truth to shape how you view yourself and that He would give you the strength to love your enemies.

The Power: *Luke 8*

In Luke 8:40-56, we see the record of a huge crowd that looks like Times Square on New Year's Eve. It seems that everyone in the area has begun to hear stories about Jesus' healings and miracles and wants to come see them for themselves. In this story, we see Jesus heal two women, one a 12-year-old girl on her deathbed and another who has been suffering for 12 years from the same sickness. While the little girl's father is pleading for Jesus to heal his daughter, the woman who has tried everything to get better pushes through the crowd and as a last resort reaches out to just touch Jesus' clothes, hoping that would do what nothing else could. And guess what? It works! She is healed immediately. She went from a sickly outcast of society to being restored by Jesus and publicly recognized for her faith in front of everyone.

As this happens, news that the 12-year-old girl has died comes to Jesus. Knowing what her daddy's reaction would be, Jesus tells him, "Don't be afraid." Jesus is about to show that He has power over even death. He goes to the girl's house, asks her to get up, and instantly she comes back to life.

Both the woman's illness and the little girl's death are a result of our sin and the curse which followed. Jesus came to defeat sin and death and reverse everything that has gone wrong as a result. In this story, we see a glimpse of what will one day be when sickness and death are defeated and gone. The woman had looked everywhere for healing and everyone thought that death was the end, but Jesus shows He is able to overcome them both. All we have to do is trust Him and we will discover His great healing power.

Think

How have you seen Jesus change and heal things in your life, whether it be a physical healing (sickness, etc.) or a relational healing (parents, siblings, etc.)? If this is hard for you to answer, try to think of a time you have asked Jesus to change or heal anything?

Spend some time thinking of people in your life, friends, classmates and family, that could benefit from Jesus' healing. Write down their names and their needs and take some time over the next week to pray for them.

Pray

Though we can't actually reach out and touch Jesus as the woman did in Luke 8, we have access to His healing power through prayer. Through prayer, we can go to God on behalf of others and ourselves. Continue to pray this week for the people you identified as you reflected earlier. Believe on their behalf that God would draw them near and would heal them.

Look at the Birds: *Luke 12*

Fear is one of the biggest hindrances to following Christ. It takes many shapes and forms: worry, peer pressure, stress, anxiety and even racism. It is something none of us are free from. We all struggle with it in one way or another. Knowing this was a huge problem for people then and now, Jesus responds to it in His teaching in Luke 12:22-34. Jesus, in order to show how much God is in control, looks at the life of a bird. It never goes to the store, it never plans a meal, it doesn't worry about any of this, yet it still lives as God provides for it. Jesus is reminding us that God is in control of His creation. He then points to a flower and how beautiful they are though they have done nothing to make themselves that way. Again, God takes care of His creation. Jesus then argues, if God cares enough to take care of something as small as birds and flowers, how much more will God take care of us, human beings who were called "very good" when He made us!

What sense does it then make for us to worry? If God is in control and taking care of us, what do we have to worry about? Instead, we are free to set our minds on Christ's Kingdom and His Mission. If God saved us at the cost of His only son, how will He not take care of our other less significant needs?

Think

What things in your life do you worry most about? Think about them and write them down.

The gospel teaches us that the love of Christ is what takes away our stress and worry. How does knowing that take away the worry you have about the things listed above? Mark through the things listed above as you pray that God would take the worry you have with them away.

Pray

Turn to and read Philippians 4:4-7. Paul tells us how to live a life free from worry and fear. Pray. Pray often. Pray always. Don't every stop praying. When you feel anxiety coming into your life, turn to God and ask Him to take it away. God promises that He will give us a peace just like the one Christ Himself has. Begin by asking God for a peace against fear and anxiety in your life now.

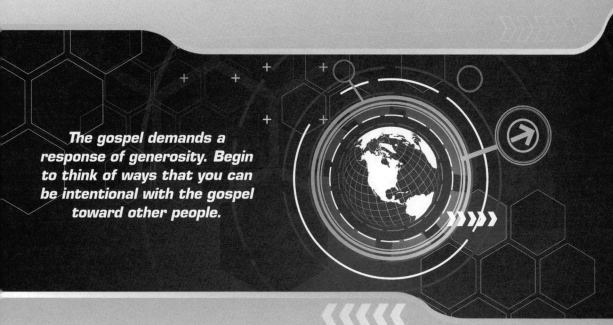

The gospel demands a response of generosity. Begin to think of ways that you can be intentional with the gospel toward other people.

Is your life marked more by generosity or selfishness?

SESSION 6:
GOSPEL FAITH

"As I pray, I'll measure your compassion by the cross and your power by the resurrection." The Gospel Prayer, Part 4

In the early 1990s, God was beginning to move greatly in the hearts of a few key people on college campuses all across the nation and across the globe. In 1995, a movement was launched: Passion. Passion has had one mission for more than twenty years; to call college students to live for the name and renown of Christ among the nations. What started off as a few thousand college students gathering at the first conference outside of Austin, Texas, has now grown into a global movement that has reached millions of students on every continent for the glory of Christ.

If you're anything like me, you're probably thinking, "how does something like that happen?". It's pretty simple. Someone believed God was willing and able to send revival to our world, they asked God to send it, and they acted as if He would.

That same pattern takes place throughout the Book of Acts. Acts is the story of a group of disciples who believed that Jesus loves sinners as much as the gospel shows that He does. God uses the prayers of believers to unleash His power on the world. That's exactly what God desires from each one of us: belief.

Warm Up

When you think about prayer, what are the top five things that come to your mind? What is one thing that stands out to you the most about what you have been taught about prayer?

Think back to some unexpected good things that you have experienced in this past year. Do you think that prayer may have played a role? If so, explain.

Weekly Review

Part 3 of the Gospel Prayer expresses our reaction to God's love toward us. We love others because of the way we've experienced God's love towards us in Christ. Jason talked about how the gospel motivates us because of grace rather than by guilt. We studied the early church in Acts and how their generosity was contagious to the on-looking community that God had placed them in.

When you look over the past five weeks of reading, what themes or patterns stand out to you? What picture of Jesus most clearly comes to mind?

When we ended our session last week, we developed a game plan to show off the generosity of Christ to those in your schools/circles of influence. Did you have the opportunity to carry that out this week? If so, please share.

Video Set Up

In Session 6, we move into the last part of the Gospel Prayer. Jason will unpack what the biggest obstacle to seeing God do great things in our lives and around us tends to be, and open up our eyes to the power and compassion that flows from the God of the universe when we respond in belief.

Video Guide: SESSION 6 "Gospel Faith"

The biggest obstacle to seeing God do great things is our

_____.

Matthew 13:58

Unbelief is rejecting the _____ that God declares and seeking

_____ in something else.

As I _____, I will measure your _____ by the

cross and your power by the _____.

God's supply of compassion is always _____.

When your mind starts to doubt and go into unbelief, always redirect your mind and your heart back to the _____.

Video Feedback

The goal here is to talk about the video and to enhance your experience by hearing how God is using this teaching in the lives of others in your group.

How does this teaching encourage you to pray differently than you did before?

If you could summarize the key point of this message in a tweet, what would it be?

Have you ever taken a dare on the compassion and power of God like the woman in Luke 8? Share your experience with the group.

How does the fact that God's power and compassion supply never runs out change the way you pray?

Come up with a tweetable key point, and when your group is finished meeting, tweet/update your Facebook status with that key phrase (using the hashtag "#gospelrev").

Discussion Questions

1. When you pray, how would you categorize your attitude when you approach God? Reluctant? Unbelieving? Bold? Explain with the group.

2. Read Mark 1:40-42 and Luke 11:11-13. How does the way the man with the disease approached Jesus, and Jesus' response, set for us a model for the way we pray? How does it compare to your prayer life right now?

3. 1 John 5:14-15 tells us that if we ask according to the will of God, we will have our prayers answered. What does this say about the nature of prayer?

4. Read James 5:13-18. This passage tells us about the importance of praying as a community of believers. If this passage really is instructing us to pray with others, how does it challenge your current prayer life?

5. What are some action steps you can put in place this week to begin praying with other people? Share your thoughts with the group.

Wrap Up

In this session, we explored the core element of a gospel-centered prayer life: belief! We've seen that God is both compassionate and powerful when it comes to our prayers. The more Christ's desires become our desires, the more our prayers become catalysts for unleashing His power in the world. Prayer is meant to be practiced in community as well as in your personal life. It should be a common practice for believers to pray over one another and actually see God do miraculous things in each other's lives.

When was the last time you saw something miraculous happen in someone's life that you were praying for? If you can't think of a time, examine your heart to determine if unbelief could be damaging your relationship with Christ.

Pray

In your prayer time today, take a few minutes and pray specifically over a few requests that someone in your group may have. Remember, God's compassion and His power are always full, and He wants to answer your prayers as they align with His good and perfect will. Ask boldly and with confidence. Write your prayer below and continue praying this prayer daily until you see God's hand moving in the situation.

Worth It: *Luke 14*

Ever thought about starting your own religion? Okay, so that is a weird question. But, hey, let's conduct our own little thought experiment with this (we might even learn something!). What would you promise your followers to get them "in"? Wealth- definitely. Happiness- absolutely. Satisfaction-certainly. What about hatred of your family? What about lugging around a torture device?

Look at Luke 14:25-33 again. Then think- why does Jesus require these things of His disciples? Maybe Jesus knows something we don't. Maybe He knows that those who think following Him will be easy will stop when it gets hard. Maybe He knows that for some of them, a torture device really did stand in their future. Maybe He knew that unless His followers gave up everything to follow Him, they wouldn't have room to receive all of His blessings!

Let's be real, being a disciple is tough. And to be honest, you wouldn't want it any other way. No really, think about it. The only God worth giving everything to is the God who requires everything you have. Genesis 1 and 2 tells us that you were created for God, and anything less than God will fail to satisfy. Jesus' hard words are gifts to you. Renouncing all we have and following Christ is like letting go of the side of the pool for the first time and experiencing the freedom of swimming in water. We cannot do both. As C.S. Lewis said in his classic, *Mere Christianity*, "Fallen man is not simply an imperfect creature who needs improvement; he is a rebel who must lay down his arms."

Think

Jesus is calling you to lay everything down under His control. To give up everything. And not just once. Romans 12:1-2 tells us that the disciple of Christ is to be a living sacrifice. Ask yourself a hard question: When you hear these words of Jesus, what is the one thing that you do not want to let go of?

Have you ever made the decision to give up everything and follow Christ? Are you holding anything back? If not, are you willing to do that now?

Pray

Jesus preaches this same message again in John 12:25, when He says that one must hate his life in this world in order to keep it in eternity. Jesus wants something from you, and that is simply: everything. He wants you to know that life is better with Him in control than you in control. Spend some time meditating over an idea. When was there a time in your life where you gave control completely to God? What happened? Can you trust God with your life? Why or why not?

Give it All: *Luke 21*

You know how it goes. You've seen it in your school cafeteria. Athletes sit with athletes. Skaters sit with skaters. Rich students sit with, well rich students. In this story in Luke 21, Jesus and His disciples are observing Jerusalem's wealthy drop money in the offering box. But then someone comes onto the scene who clearly did not fit in. A lonely, poor widow. And she put in two small copper coins. Everyone else thinks nothing of it, but Jesus was astounded.

Jesus takes this time to point out to His disciples that she put in more than all of the others. What does He mean? Surely others put in much more than this poor widow! Jesus is on to something. He is pointing out that God doesn't need our money. But He wants our hearts. This widow gave everything she had. Are we willing to do the same?

Think

You know how a car has a lot of gauges and instruments on the dashboard? These all tell you something about how the car is running. If the temperature is too hot, then something is wrong with the engine. For our spiritual lives, we have a few of these "gauges" as well. Our spending habits are certainly one of these. They reflect what we value. What does your spending say that you value most?

Think of the last three major expenses you had. Who were they for? What did they do? Do they reflect your love for the God who saved you?

What do you think the next step is? Remember, Jesus is after much more than your money. He is after your heart.

Pray

For the Christian, generosity flows out of understanding what Jesus has done. Can you believe that the God who created everything stepped out of heaven to come to a smelly stable? That He who was beautiful and strong for our sake became ugly and weak? Ask God to help you understand His generosity to you. Then reflect on how you can show that same generosity to others.

The Bread and the Cup: *Luke 22*

So Jesus does something very interesting here in Luke 22. He knows that He is going to suffer and die soon. He also knows that as soon as He does, His disciples are going to be scattered and persecuted. So, what does He do? Give them a battle plan? Construct a fortress? Plan for an evacuation? No, but He establishes a meal. This has been called the Lord's table, the Lord's Supper, the Passover meal, or communion. Different churches practice it in different ways, but its importance is agreed upon by all.

This meal was to be one of the central organizing points for Jesus' church. They were to eat together, and remember that Jesus body was broken for their sin. They were to drink together and remember His spilled blood. This was a sermon made visible.

By taking the elements of the meal, we declare to one another that we believe Jesus' death was for us and we acknowledge that we've chosen Christ. We are affirming our union with Christ together and preaching the gospel of the substitutionary (Jesus in our place) death of Christ to each other. Jesus died for our sins, in our place, so that we could believe in Him and become children of God (John 1:12-13).

Think

Why do you think Christ made a meal central to His church?

When you take the Lord's Supper, what message are you celebrating? How can you explain this to your friends?

Pray

Jesus gave the church the Lord's Supper to "remember me." Take a few moments to remember Jesus. Remember what He did for you, and what He does for you. Remember that His body was broken, and his blood was poured out. Offer thanks to God for His salvation!

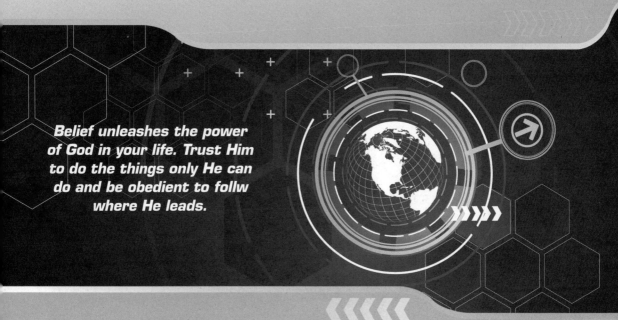

Belief unleashes the power of God in your life. Trust Him to do the things only He can do and be obedient to follw where He leads.

Are you trusting God to do great things in and through you or is your life dominated by unbelief?

SUBSTITUTE GOSPELS

"We never grow beyond the gospel, we just grow deeper into the gospel."

A couple of years ago I was tasked with planting blueberry bushes in my backyard. It was my first shot at being a gardener other than the time we attempted to grow tomato plants in a cup in 3rd grade. The blueberry bushes proved to be a bit more difficult than I had expected. Planting the bushes was one thing, but tending to them was another! Taking care of plants is a slow process and it doesn't happen overnight. It took a lot of watering, pulling weeds, and most of all: patience. You see, the blueberries didn't come in a week. In fact, the blueberries didn't come until the next year. It took time to produce the fruit I was hoping would be produced. That's a difficult thing to grasp considering the fast-paced culture that we live in. When we want something, we download an app on our phone and have it immediately.

Parallels to our spiritual lives abound. The care of planting bushes is remarkably similar to the care a new Christian needs. The constant pulling of weeds to keep the bushes from being choked out is just like the battle against sin that we face in our lives. If the bush is healthy, it grows fruit. If the bush is not healthy, no matter what you do, it will not produce the fruit you want it to produce.

Often, we get so excited about getting to the next stage of our spiritual lives that we forget the one thing we need to survive: the gospel! The gospel is not a stage we pass through. It's the one thing we need in every stage of our lives. No matter how mature of a Christian we think we are, if we don't have the gospel, we are dead. God is the soil of our growth and the gospel is the water.

Warm Up

Have you ever planted anything and had to take care of it (yes, Chia® pets count)? What was the experience like?

When you're not growing in your spiritual life, what are some of the biggest factors keeping you from growing?

Weekly Review

Last week you worked through the last part of the Gospel Prayer, which says "As I pray, I'll measure Your compassion by the cross and Your power by the resurrection." In the video, Jason talked about the fact that the biggest obstacle we face in seeing God do great things in our lives is not the lack of resources your youth ministry may have or your lack of knowledge of the Scriptures. Simply put: it's your unbelief.

How has your prayer life been impacted this past week as a result of being challenged to pray in belief in God's compassion and power?

You've been challenged to read through the Gospels and you've read a lot of Scripture up to this point. Has any story or particular passage stuck out to you along the way? What have been some things that you have been doing to help you remember the things you are reading?

Video Set Up

In this session, Jason will unpack ways that we make secondary things in our lives the primary thing and how this is detrimental to our growth as believers. Jason will give you a few examples of how we often approach Scripture with secondary things in mind, rather than primary things and how the gospel changes our approach to studying the Bible. Be sure and pay close attention to what Jason says the goal of a sermon should be.

Video Guide: Session 7: "Substitute Gospels"

1. Paul spoke frequently about "secondary things," but he always focused on the primary thing: the gospel. The gospel supplies the _____ to accomplish all the other things.

2. "Always plow a _____ back to the gospel." —Charles Spurgeon
Explain what this quote means in your own words and why it is important.

3. The gospel is the power behind all of our _____ _____.

4. The goal of a lecture is to leave with information. The goal of a motivational speech is to leave with action steps. The goal of a sermon is to leave _____. —D. Martyn Lloyd Jones

Video Feedback

The goal here is to talk about the video and to enhance your experience by hearing how God is using this teaching in the lives of others in your group.

In what ways have you made primary things secondary? What is the major danger with doing this?

How does your church and youth group model "gospel-centrality?" Would you say the gospel is central to the members of your church?

If you could summarize the key point in this message in a tweet, what would it be?

Take a minute or two and share that thought with your friends. Tweet/ update your Facebook status with that key phrase (using the hashtag "#gospelrev").

Jason shared that D. Martyn Lloyd Jones once explained the goal of a lecture is to leave with information. The goal of a motivational speech is to leave with actions steps. The goal of a sermon is to leave worshiping. How does that change the way you listen to sermons and read your Bible?

Discussion Questions

1. Read 1 Corinthians 2:2. Did Paul actually want them to know nothing except for Jesus and Him crucified? Paul is definitely trying to make a point, so let's start there. What is the reason you think Paul might be so emphatic about this statement?

2. Galatians 6:14-15 also explores the idea that other things pale in comparison to the gospel. Paul is talking about a divisive issue (circumcision) that had become a pretty big deal in the life of the church. Why does Paul say this is not important anymore? What are some relevant examples today of how we do this in our churches?

3. Read 1 Timothy 6:20-21. Paul tells Timothy to make sure he guards the gospel that has been entrusted to him. Why do you think this is important? How can you put up safeguards in your life to help you from falling away from the beauty of the gospel?

4. What are some things you can do alongside others in your group to make sure that you are not forgetting the gospel? Share your thoughts with the group.

5. Read Galatians 3:1-3. In this passage, Paul is rebuking the Galatians for trying to justify themselves based on what they do when they were already justified based on what Christ did. Paul is so surprised that he begins to jokingly ask them who has hypnotized them. How do we slip into this same trap? Describe a time when this has happened in your life.

6. How are Paul's words of rebuke helpful for us as we fight against adding things to the gospel like the Galatians were doing?

Wrap Up

In this session, we looked at just how easy it is to get caught up in secondary things and make them primary. Jason gave us some great examples of how we often approach Scripture not looking to find more of the beauty of God in the gospel, but for ways we can become better people. Remember, the gospel changes everything, even the way we change!

Pray

Take some time and write a prayer asking God to reveal the beauty of the gospel in fresh ways every day of your life. Pray that you will never get over the gospel, but you will instead go deeper in it.

The Gospel According to John: *John 3*

So you may have never heard of the verse, John 3:16. Or you may have. You might be able to recite it in your head without even thinking about what it means. We are going to camp here on John 3:16-21. As you read, emphasize a few different words in your head. Say them louder as you read. Try these: God, world, believe, life.

Let's play a brief word game. When you read *world* in this verse, what do you always think of? If you are like me, you probably think of people. But do you want to know something that might change the way you think of the gospel? The word here is cosmos. What do you think of when you hear the word cosmos? Well, you think of everything. Earth, seas, animals, people, stars, planets, air, light—everything. Now read John 3:16 again. God came to save what? Everything!

God is working to restore ALL things to Himself, people being chief among them. This passage also uses the continued metaphor of light and darkness. The light exposes things, the darkness hides it. If we have nothing to hide, we have no fear of the light. If we have things to hide, darkness is more attractive. Jesus wants to get you and I to a point where we have nothing to hide. No sin. No guilt. Just glorious transparency and freedom.

Think

How does God's mission to save the cosmos change your view of salvation?

What role do you think believers have in light and darkness? Is it easy to expose things that are hiding in the darkness?

What about you? Is there anything in your life that you are hiding? Do you feel a weight or a burden just thinking about it? Write down one thing below that you want to give to God and not carry anymore.

Pray

This whole gospel story began with God creating a planet and a world that He pronounced, "good". Then sin entered the world and not only mankind, but the whole earth, is cursed. John 3:16 tells us that God is working to not only restore humanity, but the earth as well! Give glory to God for His wonderful blessing. Think of part of creation that you find most beautiful and praise God for it. Ask God what He would have you do in light of His global mission.

Jesus is Bigger: *John 6*

When kings or emperors came into their kingdom, they would often introduce their reign with a demonstration of what type of king they were (think of Rehoboam in 2 Chronicles 10). Think of Roman emperors who gave out food to the people and hosted games in the Colosseum. This meant that they were going to be rulers who wanted the people to love them. Other kings would crucify or execute rebels as a statement that they would be harsh and cruel rulers. Some would even display the bodies on the city walls.

Now think about Jesus. He too is a king coming into a kingdom. What was the first miracle He did? He turned water into wine (John 2). The coming of Jesus to earth was one of joy and merriment. Jesus makes another grand statement about what kind of king He is going to be by feeding well over five thousand people!

Now things take a turn the following day. People come running after Jesus again, because (1) the food was free and (2) if Jesus made it, you know it was some good food. What is His response in John 6:25-27? To paraphrase, "physical food is good and necessary, but do not seek it at the expense of spiritual food." You see, our greatest need is not things (even good things) from God, but God Himself! Consider Romans 8:32, "He did not even spare His own Son but offered Him up for us all; how will He not also with Him grant us everything?"

Think

So, let's be real. We usually pray to God to get things from Him, not for God Himself. We are like children who are excited about the arrival of our father from a business trip because we know he will bring us toys. Write down two things that you find yourself asking God for most often.

In what ways do you need the presence of God rather than His gifts?

What is going on in your life for which you are not yet trusting in the power of Christ?

Pray

John 6 is not a promise that God will provide for every craving we may have. But it is a demonstration that He can take even the smallest things and multiply them to meet our needs. What are your needs? Have you been believing that God can provide for them, even out of small resources? Pray and ask God for the provision of your needs. Ask Him to give you a heart of gratitude for the things that He has so richly provided.

Dying to Live: *John 12*

Have you ever heard of *Band of Brothers*? The series chronicles the journey of a unit of soldiers who fight numerous battles during the European campaign of World War II. In each battle, they have to entrust their lives to one another as they work together to win.

There's one scene that stands out in particular. A young soldier is having trouble doing everything he needs to do in battle. He is hesitant, skittish, and unprepared in combat. One of the seasoned veterans (picture Chuck Norris in camo) sits the young guy down and breaks things down for him. He tells him the only reason he is scared is because he is trying to hold on to his life. He doesn't realize he is already dead. Once this soldier counts his life as over, he is not longer worried about what happens to himself. He can commit fully to his unit and to battle.

In John 12:20-26, Jesus makes a remarkably similar point. If one loves his life here in this world, he will not be able to follow Christ. One of the continuing things you should be hearing over and over again in this study is that Jesus requires everything from His followers. They can hold nothing back. They must die to themselves to follow him. If Jesus is Lord over only part of your life, He is Lord of none of it. He is like a vice president. You are still the president. But once we consider our lives over, then we can truly begin to live like God designed us to live. There is a sort of glorious release that happens.

Think

It's really easy for people to give up control of their lives to Christ right? No! It's difficult. What areas in your life are the most difficult?

Dying to self is not something that happens once and for all. Rather, it begins once and continues. But we have to make firm decisions to follow Jesus every day. But let's be honest: a God who is not worthy of everything probably isn't worth very much.

Pray

Read Philippians 3:17-21. Here, the apostle Paul makes an amazing claim that knowing Jesus is better than anything else the world has to offer. Have you ever thought of how anyone could give up all the pleasures of this world to follow Jesus? Could it be that they have discovered a better pleasure than anything else in the world? Ask God to open your eyes to worship Him. Ask Him to be better in your sight than everything else the world has to offer.

The gospel must be primary. If we aren't careful, our lives can become filled with secondary things that we give primary importance to. Spend some time evaluating your priorities this week.

What things have you allowed to take precedence over the gospel?

GOSPEL DEPTH

"Christian growth is not usually learning something new, but going deeper in what you already know. Many of us know gospel doctrines, but we've never been ravished by them."

Here we are. The final week of this eight week trek called the *Gospel Revolution*. I hope it has sparked something wonderful in you along the way. I hope the gospel is beginning to stir an awakening in your soul that is unsettling the rhythms of your life. God, through the gospel, has been renovating every corner of my life, and He isn't finished yet. The deeper I go into the gospel, the more I find myself changed by it.

I hope this will be your story as well. And I hope it isn't just your story, but the story of the church in this era. The reality is that the church is at a crossroads. In the next 50 years the church in the English-speaking world will look drastically different than it does right now. Either it will continue the decline it is on, or a new awakening will occur that will bring with it salvation and hope in a wave that has not been seen in three generations. I believe the latter can happen and it will begin when we individually and corporately begin to immerse ourselves in the gospel.

Warm Up

What moment over the past eight weeks sticks out to you as a landmark for your group and why? Maybe it's an "aha" or a "ha ha" moment or something else altogether. Describe your moment.

When you think of major turning points in your life, what role has the gospel played? What role do you hope it will play in the future? Explain.

Weekly Review

Last week the group looked at how we try to create substitutes for the gospel. We alter the gospel as God gave it to us to fit our wants and needs, unintentionally (usually) turning God more into a butler than a sovereign King. Error, you may have heard, is truth out of proportion. There are many movements across the Christian landscape today that are guilty of taking truth out of proportion and as a result leading people away from the power that resides in the gospel.

John's Gospel is clearly a different style than the other three. What metaphor about Christ spoke most clearly to your mind and perhaps left an unforgettable impression on your heart?

Did God remind you of Paul's words (the gospel is of first importance) in your life this past week? If so, in what ways?

Video Set Up

In this final session, J.D. is pointing us to a familiar story in Scripture, the story of Jesus and Zacchaeus, to show how the gospel of Jesus creates in us a completely new person when we encounter it. This session also serves as a summary for the big ideas woven throughout the past seven sessions. The gospel, when rightly understood, overwhelms us and changes us permanently. As you listen to J.D. talk through how that process has taken place in his own life, consider how Christ is changing you.

Video Guide: SESSION 8: "Gospel Depth"

The gospel changes you not by _____ but by _____ your heart with God's love.

1. Jesus extended _____ to Zacchaeus when _____ _____ else would.

2. Jesus called him out of a place of _____ down into _____ with Him.

Growth in Christ never happens by going beyond the _____(gospel), but rather by going deeper into the gospel.

Video Feedback

The goal here is to talk about the video and to enhance your experience by hearing how God is using this teaching in the lives of others in your group.

How would you summarize J.D.'s message to the group in this last session?

You've heard and read how Jesus changed and is changing so many lives. How is Jesus changing you? To which biblical figure can you best relate? Explain.

Have you ever experienced grace extended to you from someone you least expected? Share your experience with the group.

We all, like Zaccheus, have experienced radical grace from Christ. How does that grace extended to you cause you to extend grace to others?

What is one thought from the video you think your friends need to hear? Come up with a tweetable key point to share with your friends. Either tweet or update your Facebook status with that key phrase (using the hashtag "#gospelrev"). You may also want to search Twitter using the #gospelrev hashtag to see what others are saying.

Discussion Questions

1. Read Isaiah 53:3-5 and 1 Peter 1:10-12. The prophet Isaiah is looking forward to the coming Messiah. Underline words that describe this Messiah. In what ways did Jesus fulfill this prophecy?

2. How do Peter's words help us understand the gospel that was foretold in Isaiah? What do you think Peter intended by introducing angels into the conversation?

Now that you've begun to understand the weight the Scriptures puts on the gospel, let's complete the discussion by looking forward to how we will now live.

3. Read Galatians 1:6-10. Paul is emphatic that we not allow ourselves to be swayed by another gospel. How do you think we can know a false gospel when we hear it? How does that differ from the substitute gospels we looked at last week? Explain.

4. Read Acts 1:7-11. What do you think is your role in this great story of God? How can you and your church engage in this gospel mission?

5. Notice in Acts 1:10-11 the disciples are still looking up into heaven when the two men in white clothes correct them and tell them to get to work. Why do you think the author makes a point to add this little section in? What should we glean from it about our own lives as followers of Christ?

6. How has what you've learned in this study encouraged you in your own gospel revolution? Explain.

Wrap Up

This session summarized and reemphasized the core themes expounded upon over the past eight weeks. J.D. showed us through the encounter between Jesus and Zacchaeus that the gospel changes everything. When we encounter Christ we must respond. We can either reject Him as some have done or worship Him as others have. What we cannot do is ignore Him. The more we immerse ourselves in the gospel, the more God's power is unleashed in us and the more we change into the image of Christ. We are the people of the gospel who have been given the power of the Holy Spirit to make this good news known throughout the world.

Pray

Over the course of the previous eight weeks, you've been challenged in many ways. Everything from the way you view religion and the gospel, to the way you try to earn God's love (don't forget you can't earn it, but it can be gifted to you through Christ.) Rather than closing the book and walking away, spend these last few moments writing a prayer challenging yourself to embrace the love of Christ demonstrated through the gospel and to continue to wade into the depths of a gospel-centered life. Write your prayer below:

The Only Way?: *John 14*

I'll never forget the conversation for as long as I live. I just finished giving a presentation in my high school history class on how Christianity is the hope for all people in every nation. It was my first attempt at being bold in front of all my classmates with the gospel, and I felt great about the presentation. Afterward, as I left the class, one of my close friends came up to me and confronted me in the hallway and said "Do you really think that the people who die without hearing about Jesus will go to hell? Don't you think that is a pretty arrogant thing to say? If you believe that to be true, we can't be friends."

In John 14, Jesus makes it very clear that there is no way to the Father other than through Him. Jesus tells His disciples that to see Him is to see God the Father. Acts 4:12 tells us that there is no other name than Jesus by which men can be saved. The gospel is the way—the only way—to be saved. If we believe this great truth, it doesn't make us arrogant, it makes us humble and active. The nations need Jesus, and it is our joy and mission to make His name known among them.

Think

If Jesus really is the only way to heaven, how does that impact the way you respond to Him?

In what ways can you be involved in the church's effort to reach others for Christ? How can you encourage your youth group to be about this mission?

Pray

When you really consider the weight of the claim that the gospel you've been studying for eight weeks really is the only way to be saved, you should begin to be burdened for those who have not yet heard. As you pray today, pray for God to bring people in your life that do not know Christ to salvation. Ask God to give you boldness and humility as you go about telling people of His salvation. Also, take a moment and pray for an unreached people group around the world. If you don't know of any, consult someone on your church staff or you can check out *www.operationworld.org* or visit *www.imb.org* and click on "Pray" for a list of those people groups and how to pray for them.

The King of the Jews: *John 19*

If you've ever seen the movie, *The Passion of the Christ*, you know that the crucifixion of Jesus was much more intense than our minds will allow us to imagine. John 19, much like other passages that describe the crucifixion of Jesus, is an intense passage. The passage is broken down into three segments

- The sentencing (vv. 1-16)

- The crucifixion (vv. 17-27)

- The death and burial (vv. 28-42)

When we think about the gospel we often focus on Jesus on the cross and forget the road He took to it. Let's not forget, the road wasn't pretty. Pilate, though he found no guilt in Jesus, sentenced him to death. Jesus was beaten badly and given a crown of thorns that pierced through the skin on His skull and tore His face to pieces. He was mocked, spit on, and eventually handed over to his accusers. Jesus, bloody and beaten, carried the heavy cross beam for His own cross to the distant place where they would eventually kill Him. Once there, they took long nails and drove them into His hands and nailed Him to the tree.

Are you getting this scene? It's a brutal and bloody scene. After some time, Jesus gave up His spirit, dying at the hands of the very people He came to save. This is our Savior: dead on a tree. His disciples buried Him, the tomb was enclosed with a stone, and guards were placed around it. Hope seemed to have been lost.

We cannot let the events of John 19 just go in one ear and out the other. We need to allow the agony Christ endured to sit on our hearts and minds. If we want to understand Christ's love, we must begin to understand His pain.

Think

What emotional reaction does the pain Jesus went through during His trial and crucifixion create in you? Why?

The death of Jesus puts on display the compassion and love of God for you. How is God creating a life of thanksgiving for the cross in your life?

Pray

This one is simple. Jesus died the death that we deserved to die. He was the payment for God's wrath on our behalf. Jesus' love is sacrificial and it's for you. Thank Him for dying on that cross in your place. Worship Jesus for atoning for your sin!

So That You May Believe...And Live!: *John 20*

We've all been asked by our English teachers to make sure that we are identifying the thesis statements of the stories we are reading for class. That's because every story has a point and if you don't get the point, you've missed the boat.

Chapter 20 in John's Gospel seems to give us great insight on the point of the story he has just painted for us in the previous nineteen chapters. It is this:

> [30]Jesus performed many other signs in the presence of His disciples that are not written in this book. [31]But these are written so that you may believe Jesus is the Messiah, the Son of God, and by believing you may have life in His name.

Did you catch that? The whole point of the gospel of John is that by believing that Jesus is who He says He is, you gain life that comes through that belief. John doesn't just want to give you a bunch of information to fill your mind. He wants to give you great truth that will bring about life for you!

This chapter is filled with appearances of Christ. Jesus' resurrection declared His victory over death and He wanted His disciples to know it. So He appeared to them quite a few times. Yet Jesus says we who believe through the hearing of the gospel message are even more blessed. The purpose of this eight-week trek through these four books is really summed up in John's statement. The more we come to believe the gospel, the more we experience the life for which we were created.

Think

Jesus is still performing signs in the presence of His disciples. In what ways has Jesus displayed His great love for you recently?

What specific things are you walking away with from this Bible study experience? Be sure to share some of these takeaways with your friends.

Pray

The resurrection changes everything. Because Jesus got up out of the grave, you and I have victory over death! We have new life that is found in Christ. This is what makes the gospel great news. Spend some time thanking God for Jesus' resurrection and its implications for your life. Thank Him for the gospel and for the life you get to experience because of it.

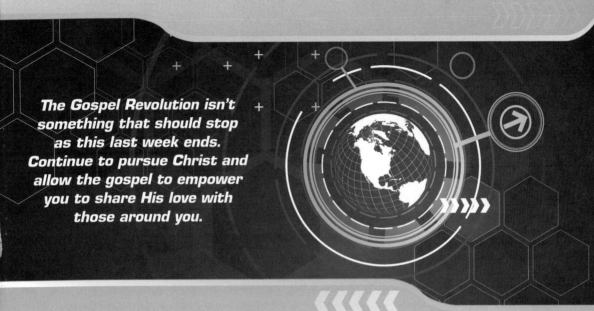

The Gospel Revolution isn't something that should stop as this last week ends. Continue to pursue Christ and allow the gospel to empower you to share His love with those around you.

What are five thoughts that have impacted you the most during this study?

Write them here so you can remember them.

NOTES: